LET THE

Adventure

BEGIN →→

These are the Adventures of:

_____

_____

_____

Dates: _____

⛰ _____

Date: _____ Start Time: _____ End Time: _____

Weather: ☀ 🌙 ☁ 🌧 ⛈ 🌨 Temps: _____ Wind: _____

City/State/Country: _____

Trail(s)/Park: _____

Terrain: _____

Facilities: _____

Costs/Fees: _____

Cell Reception/Carrier: _____

Trail Type: out/back   loop   one way/shuttle

Start Latitude/Longitude: _____

End Longitude/Latitude: _____

Elevation Gain/Loss: _____

Total Time: _____   Total Distance: _____

Trail Conditions: _____

Hiking Party: _____

_____

Significant Observations: _____

_____

Hike Rating: ☆ ☆ ☆ ☆ ☆

Gear Thoughts:

_____

_____

Food Thoughts:

_____

_____

Other Notes

_____

_____

_____

_____

_____

_____

_____

_____

_____

_____

_____

_____

_____

_____

Date:_____ Start Time:_____ End Time:_____

Weather: ☀ 🌙 🌧 ⛈ 🌨   Temps: Wind:

City/State/Country:_____

Trail(s)/Park:_____

Terrain:_____

Facilities:_____

Costs/Fees:_____

Cell Reception/Carrier:_____

Trail Type: out/back   loop   one way/shuttle

Start Latitude/Longitude:_____

End Longitude/Latitude:_____

Elevation Gain/Loss:_____

Total Time:_____ Total Distance:_____

Trail Conditions:_____

Hiking Party:_____

_____

Significant Observations:_____

_____

Hike Rating: ☆ ☆ ☆ ☆ ☆

Gear Thoughts:_____

_____

_____

Food Thoughts:_____

_____

_____

Other Notes

_____

_____

_____

_____

_____

_____

_____

_____

_____

_____

_____

_____

_____

_____

_____

_____

Date:_____ Start Time:_____ End Time:_____

Weather: ☀ ☾ ☁ ⚡ ❄   Temps:_____ Wind:_____

City/State/Country:_____

Trail(s)/Park:_____

Terrain:_____

Facilities:_____

Costs/Fees:_____

Cell Reception/Carrier:_____

Trail Type: out/back   loop   one way/shuttle

Start Latitude/Longitude:_____

End Longitude/Latitude:_____

Elevation Gain/Loss:_____

Total Time:_____ Total Distance:_____

Trail Conditions:_____

Hiking Party:_____

_____

Significant Observations:_____

_____

Hike Rating: ☆ ☆ ☆ ☆ ☆

Gear Thoughts:_____

_____

_____

Food Thoughts:_____

_____

_____

Other Notes

_____

_____

_____

_____

_____

_____

_____

_____

_____

_____

_____

_____

_____

_____

_____

Date:_____ Start Time:_____ End Time:_____

Weather: ☀ 🌙 🌧 ⚡ ❄   Temps:_____ Wind:_____

City/State/Country:_____

Trail(s)/Park:_____

Terrain:_____

Facilities:_____

Costs/Fees:_____

Cell Reception/Carrier:_____

Trail Type: out/back   loop   one way/shuttle

Start Latitude/Longitude:_____

End Longitude/Latitude:_____

Elevation Gain/Loss:_____

Total Time:_____ Total Distance:_____

Trail Conditions:_____

Hiking Party:_____
_____

Significant Observations:_____
_____

Hike Rating: ☆☆☆☆☆

Gear Thoughts: _____
_____
_____

Food Thoughts: _____
_____
_____

Other Notes

Date:_____ Start Time:_____ End Time:_____

Weather: ☀ 🌤 🌧 ⛈ 🌨 Temps: Wind:

City/State/Country:_____

Trail(s)/Park:_____

Terrain:_____

Facilities:_____

Costs/Fees:_____

Cell Reception/Carrier:_____

Trail Type: out/back loop one way/shuttle

Start Latitude/Longitude:_____

End Longitude/Latitude:_____

Elevation Gain/Loss:_____

Total Time:_____ Total Distance:_____

Trail Conditions:_____

Hiking Party:_____
_____

Significant Observations:_____
_____

Hike Rating: ☆☆☆☆☆

Gear Thoughts: _____

_____

Food Thoughts: _____

_____

Other Notes

_____

_____

_____

_____

_____

_____

_____

_____

_____

_____

_____

_____

_____

_____

_____

_____

△△ _____

Date: _____ Start Time: _____ End Time: _____

Weather: ☀ 🌤 🌧 ⛈ 🌨 Temps: _____ Wind: _____

City/State/Country: _____

Trail(s)/Park: _____

Terrain: _____

Facilities: _____

Costs/Fees: _____

Cell Reception/Carrier: _____

Trail Type:　　　out/back　　　loop　　　one way/shuttle

Start Latitude/Longitude: _____

End Longitude/Latitude: _____

Elevation Gain/Loss: _____

Total Time: _____ Total Distance: _____

Trail Conditions: _____

Hiking Party: _____

_____

Significant Observations: _____

_____

Hike Rating: ☆ ☆ ☆ ☆ ☆

Gear Thoughts:

Food Thoughts:

Other Notes

Date:_____ Start Time:_____ End Time:_____

Weather: ☀ ☾ ☁ ☔ ⚡ ❄   Temps:_____ Wind:_____

City/State/Country:_____

Trail(s)/Park:_____

Terrain:_____

Facilities:_____

Costs/Fees:_____

Cell Reception/Carrier:_____

Trail Type: out/back   loop   one way/shuttle

Start Latitude/Longitude:_____

End Longitude/Latitude:_____

Elevation Gain/Loss:_____

Total Time:_____ Total Distance:_____

Trail Conditions:_____

Hiking Party:_____

_____

Significant Observations:_____

_____

Hike Rating: ☆☆☆☆☆

Gear Thoughts: _____

_____

Food Thoughts: _____

_____

Other Notes

Date:_____ Start Time:_____ End Time:_____

Weather: ☀ 🌙 🌧 ⚡ ❄ Temps: Wind:

City/State/Country:_____

Trail(s)/Park:_____

Terrain:_____

Facilities:_____

Costs/Fees:_____

Cell Reception/Carrier:_____

Trail Type: out/back loop one way/shuttle

Start Latitude/Longitude:_____

End Longitude/Latitude:_____

Elevation Gain/Loss:_____

Total Time:_____ Total Distance:_____

Trail Conditions:_____

Hiking Party:_____

Significant Observations:_____

Hike Rating: ☆☆☆☆☆

Gear Thoughts: _____

_____

Food Thoughts: _____

_____

Other Notes

Date:_____ Start Time:_____ End Time:_____

Weather: ☀ 🌙 🌧 ⚡ ❄   Temps: Wind:

City/State/Country:_____

Trail(s)/Park:_____

Terrain:_____

Facilities:_____

Costs/Fees:_____

Cell Reception/Carrier:_____

Trail Type: out/back   loop   one way/shuttle

Start Latitude/Longitude:_____

End Longitude/Latitude:_____

Elevation Gain/Loss:_____

Total Time:_____ Total Distance:_____

Trail Conditions:_____

Hiking Party:_____

Significant Observations:_____

Hike Rating: ☆☆☆☆☆

Gear Thoughts: _____

_____

_____

Food Thoughts: _____

_____

_____

Other Notes

Date:_____ Start Time:_____ End Time:_____

Weather: ☀ 🌙 🌧 ⚡ ❄ Temps:_____ Wind:_____

City/State/Country:_____

Trail(s)/Park:_____

Terrain:_____

Facilities:_____

Costs/Fees:_____

Cell Reception/Carrier:_____

Trail Type: out/back   loop   one way/shuttle

Start Latitude/Longitude:_____

End Longitude/Latitude:_____

Elevation Gain/Loss:_____

Total Time:_____ Total Distance:_____

Trail Conditions:_____

Hiking Party:_____
_____

Significant Observations:_____
_____

Hike Rating: ☆☆☆☆☆

Gear Thoughts: _____

_____

_____

Food Thoughts: _____

_____

_____

Other Notes

Date:_____ Start Time:_____ End Time:_____

Weather: ☀ 🌤 🌧 ⛈ 🌨   Temps: Wind:

City/State/Country:_____

Trail(s)/Park:_____

Terrain:_____

Facilities:_____

Costs/Fees:_____

Cell Reception/Carrier:_____

Trail Type: out/back   loop   one way/shuttle

Start Latitude/Longitude:_____

End Longitude/Latitude:_____

Elevation Gain/Loss:_____

Total Time:_____ Total Distance:_____

Trail Conditions:_____

Hiking Party:_____
_____

Significant Observations:_____
_____

Hike Rating: ☆☆☆☆☆

Gear Thoughts:

Food Thoughts:

Other Notes

Date:_____ Start Time:_____ End Time:_____

Weather: ☀ ☾ ☁ ⚡ ❄ Temps: Wind:

City/State/Country:_____

Trail(s)/Park:_____

Terrain:_____

Facilities:_____

Costs/Fees:_____

Cell Reception/Carrier:_____

Trail Type: out/back   loop   one way/shuttle

Start Latitude/Longitude:_____

End Longitude/Latitude:_____

Elevation Gain/Loss:_____

Total Time:_____ Total Distance:_____

Trail Conditions:_____

Hiking Party:_____

Significant Observations:_____

Hike Rating: ☆☆☆☆☆

Gear Thoughts: _____

_____

_____

Food Thoughts: _____

_____

_____

Other Notes

_____

_____

_____

_____

_____

_____

_____

_____

_____

_____

_____

_____

_____

_____

_____

Date:_____ Start Time:_____ End Time:_____

Weather: ☀ 🌙 🌧 ⛈ ❄ Temps:_____ Wind:_____

City/State/Country:_____

Trail(s)/Park:_____

Terrain:_____

Facilities:_____

Costs/Fees:_____

Cell Reception/Carrier:_____

Trail Type: out/back   loop   one way/shuttle

Start Latitude/Longitude:_____

End Longitude/Latitude:_____

Elevation Gain/Loss:_____

Total Time:_____ Total Distance:_____

Trail Conditions:_____

Hiking Party:_____
_____

Significant Observations:_____
_____

Hike Rating: ☆☆☆☆☆

Gear Thoughts:
_____

_____

_____

Food Thoughts:
_____

_____

_____

Other Notes

_____

_____

_____

_____

_____

_____

_____

_____

_____

_____

_____

_____

_____

_____

_____

_____

Date:_____ Start Time:_____ End Time:_____

Weather: ☀ ☾ 🌧 ⚡ ❄   Temps: Wind:

City/State/Country:_____

Trail(s)/Park:_____

Terrain:_____

Facilities:_____

Costs/Fees:_____

Cell Reception/Carrier:_____

Trail Type: out/back   loop   one way/shuttle

Start Latitude/Longitude:_____

End Longitude/Latitude:_____

Elevation Gain/Loss:_____

Total Time:_____ Total Distance:_____

Trail Conditions:_____

Hiking Party:_____

_____

Significant Observations:_____

_____

Hike Rating: ☆☆☆☆☆

Gear Thoughts:

Food Thoughts:

Other Notes

Date:_____ Start Time:_____ End Time:_____

Weather: ☀ ☾ ☁ ⚡ ❄ Temps:_____ Wind:_____

City/State/Country:_____

Trail(s)/Park:_____

Terrain:_____

Facilities:_____

Costs/Fees:_____

Cell Reception/Carrier:_____

Trail Type: out/back   loop   one way/shuttle

Start Latitude/Longitude:_____

End Longitude/Latitude:_____

Elevation Gain/Loss:_____

Total Time:_____   Total Distance:_____

Trail Conditions:_____

Hiking Party:_____
_____

Significant Observations:_____
_____

Hike Rating: ☆☆☆☆☆

Gear Thoughts: _____

_____

_____

Food Thoughts: _____

_____

_____

Other Notes

_____
_____
_____
_____
_____
_____
_____
_____
_____
_____
_____
_____
_____
_____
_____
_____
_____
_____
_____
_____

⛰ _____

Date: _____ Start Time: _____ End Time: _____

Weather: ☀ 🌤 🌧 ⛈ 🌨   Temps: _____ Wind: _____

City/State/Country: _____

Trail(s)/Park: _____

Terrain: _____

Facilities: _____

Costs/Fees: _____

Cell Reception/Carrier: _____

Trail Type: out/back   loop   one way/shuttle

Start Latitude/Longitude: _____

End Longitude/Latitude: _____

Elevation Gain/Loss: _____

Total Time: _____ Total Distance: _____

Trail Conditions: _____

Hiking Party: _____

_____

Significant Observations: _____

_____

Hike Rating: ☆ ☆ ☆ ☆ ☆

Gear Thoughts: _____

_____

_____

Food Thoughts: _____

_____

_____

Other Notes

Date:_____ Start Time:_____ End Time:_____

Weather: ☀ 🌙 🌧 ⛈ 🌨 Temps:_____ Wind:_____

City/State/Country:_____

Trail(s)/Park:_____

Terrain:_____

Facilities:_____

Costs/Fees:_____

Cell Reception/Carrier:_____

Trail Type: out/back   loop   one way/shuttle

Start Latitude/Longitude:_____

End Longitude/Latitude:_____

Elevation Gain/Loss:_____

Total Time:_____ Total Distance:_____

Trail Conditions:_____

Hiking Party:_____
_____

Significant Observations:_____
_____

Hike Rating: ☆☆☆☆☆

Gear Thoughts:_____

_____

_____

Food Thoughts:_____

_____

_____

Other Notes

_____

_____

_____

_____

_____

_____

_____

_____

_____

_____

_____

_____

_____

_____

_____

_____

⛰ _____

Date: _____ Start Time: _____ End Time: _____

Weather: ☀ 🌙 🌧 ⛈ ❄   Temps: _____ Wind: _____

City/State/Country: _____

Trail(s)/Park: _____

Terrain: _____

Facilities: _____

Costs/Fees: _____

Cell Reception/Carrier: _____

Trail Type: out/back   loop   one way/shuttle

Start Latitude/Longitude: _____

End Longitude/Latitude: _____

Elevation Gain/Loss: _____

Total Time: _____ Total Distance: _____

Trail Conditions: _____

Hiking Party: _____

_____

Significant Observations: _____

_____

Hike Rating: ☆☆☆☆☆

Gear Thoughts:

Food Thoughts:

Other Notes

Date:_____ Start Time:_____ End Time:_____

Weather: ☀ 🌙 🌧 ⛈ ❄ Temps: Wind:

City/State/Country:_____

Trail(s)/Park:_____

Terrain:_____

Facilities:_____

Costs/Fees:_____

Cell Reception/Carrier:_____

Trail Type: out/back loop one way/shuttle

Start Latitude/Longitude:_____

End Longitude/Latitude:_____

Elevation Gain/Loss:_____

Total Time:_____ Total Distance:_____

Trail Conditions:_____

Hiking Party:_____
_____

Significant Observations:_____
_____

Hike Rating: ☆☆☆☆☆

Gear Thoughts:

Food Thoughts:

Other Notes

⛰ _____

Date: _____ Start Time: _____ End Time: _____

Weather: ☀ 🌙 🌧 ⛈ ❄   Temps: _____ Wind: _____

City/State/Country: _____

Trail(s)/Park: _____

Terrain: _____

Facilities: _____

Costs/Fees: _____

Cell Reception/Carrier: _____

Trail Type: out/back   loop   one way/shuttle

Start Latitude/Longitude: _____

End Longitude/Latitude: _____

Elevation Gain/Loss: _____

Total Time: _____ Total Distance: _____

Trail Conditions: _____

Hiking Party: _____
_____

Significant Observations: _____
_____

Hike Rating: ☆ ☆ ☆ ☆ ☆

Gear Thoughts: _____

Food Thoughts: _____

Other Notes

△

Date:_____ Start Time:_____ End Time:_____

Weather: ☀ 🌙 🌧 ⛈ ❄   Temps:_____ Wind:_____

City/State/Country:_____

Trail(s)/Park:_____

Terrain:_____

Facilities:_____

Costs/Fees:_____

Cell Reception/Carrier:_____

Trail Type: out/back   loop   one way/shuttle

Start Latitude/Longitude:_____

End Longitude/Latitude:_____

Elevation Gain/Loss:_____

Total Time:_____ Total Distance:_____

Trail Conditions:_____

Hiking Party:_____
_____

Significant Observations:_____
_____

Hike Rating: ☆ ☆ ☆ ☆ ☆

Gear Thoughts:_____
_____
_____

Food Thoughts:_____
_____
_____

Other Notes

_____
_____
_____
_____
_____
_____
_____
_____
_____
_____
_____
_____
_____
_____
_____

⛰ _____

Date: _____ Start Time: _____ End Time: _____

Weather: ☀ 🌙 🌧 ⚡ ❄   Temps: _____   Wind: _____

City/State/Country: _____

Trail(s)/Park: _____

Terrain: _____

Facilities: _____

Costs/Fees: _____

Cell Reception/Carrier: _____

Trail Type: out/back   loop   one way/shuttle

Start Latitude/Longitude: _____

End Longitude/Latitude: _____

Elevation Gain/Loss: _____

Total Time: _____ Total Distance: _____

Trail Conditions: _____

Hiking Party: _____

_____

Significant Observations: _____

_____

Hike Rating: ☆ ☆ ☆ ☆ ☆

Gear Thoughts: _____

_____

_____

Food Thoughts: _____

_____

_____

Other Notes

_____

_____

_____

_____

_____

_____

_____

_____

_____

_____

_____

_____

_____

_____

⛰ _____

Date: _____ Start Time: _____ End Time: _____

Weather: ☀ 🌤 🌧 ⛈ 🌨   Temps: _____ Wind: _____

City/State/Country: _____

Trail(s)/Park: _____

Terrain: _____

Facilities: _____

Costs/Fees: _____

Cell Reception/Carrier: _____

Trail Type: out/back   loop   one way/shuttle

Start Latitude/Longitude: _____

End Longitude/Latitude: _____

Elevation Gain/Loss: _____

Total Time: _____ Total Distance: _____

Trail Conditions: _____

Hiking Party: _____
_____

Significant Observations: _____
_____

Hike Rating: ☆ ☆ ☆ ☆ ☆

Gear Thoughts:_____

_____

_____

Food Thoughts:_____

_____

_____

Other Notes

_____

_____

_____

_____

_____

_____

_____

_____

_____

_____

_____

_____

_____

_____

_____

_____

Date:_____ Start Time:_____ End Time:_____

Weather: ☀ ☁ 🌧 ⚡ ❄   Temps: Wind:

City/State/Country:_____

Trail(s)/Park:_____

Terrain:_____

Facilities:_____

Costs/Fees:_____

Cell Reception/Carrier:_____

Trail Type: out/back   loop   one way/shuttle

Start Latitude/Longitude:_____

End Longitude/Latitude:_____

Elevation Gain/Loss:_____

Total Time:_____ Total Distance:_____

Trail Conditions:_____

Hiking Party:_____
_____

Significant Observations:_____
_____

Hike Rating: ☆ ☆ ☆ ☆ ☆

Gear Thoughts:

Food Thoughts:

Other Notes

Date:_____ Start Time:_____ End Time:_____

Weather: ☀ ☾ ☁ 🌧 ⚡ ❄   Temps: Wind:

City/State/Country:_____

Trail(s)/Park:_____

Terrain:_____

Facilities:_____

Costs/Fees:_____

Cell Reception/Carrier:_____

Trail Type: out/back   loop   one way/shuttle

Start Latitude/Longitude:_____

End Longitude/Latitude:_____

Elevation Gain/Loss:_____

Total Time:_____ Total Distance:_____

Trail Conditions:_____

Hiking Party:_____
_____

Significant Observations:_____
_____

Hike Rating: ☆ ☆ ☆ ☆ ☆

Gear Thoughts:_____

_____

_____

Food Thoughts:_____

_____

_____

Other Notes

Date:_____ Start Time:_____ End Time:_____

Weather: ☀ 🌤 🌧 ⛈ 🌨   Temps:_____   Wind:_____

City/State/Country:_____

Trail(s)/Park:_____

Terrain:_____

Facilities:_____

Costs/Fees:_____

Cell Reception/Carrier:_____

Trail Type: out/back   loop   one way/shuttle

Start Latitude/Longitude:_____

End Longitude/Latitude:_____

Elevation Gain/Loss:_____

Total Time:_____   Total Distance:_____

Trail Conditions:_____

Hiking Party:_____
_____

Significant Observations:_____
_____

Hike Rating: ☆ ☆ ☆ ☆ ☆

Gear Thoughts: _____

_____

_____

Food Thoughts: _____

_____

_____

Other Notes

_____

_____

_____

_____

_____

_____

_____

_____

_____

_____

_____

_____

_____

_____

_____

_____

Date: _____ Start Time: _____ End Time: _____

Weather: ☀ 🌙 🌧 ⚡ ❄ Temps: _____ Wind: _____

City/State/Country: _____

Trail(s)/Park: _____

Terrain: _____

Facilities: _____

Costs/Fees: _____

Cell Reception/Carrier: _____

Trail Type: out/back   loop   one way/shuttle

Start Latitude/Longitude: _____

End Longitude/Latitude: _____

Elevation Gain/Loss: _____

Total Time: _____   Total Distance: _____

Trail Conditions: _____

Hiking Party: _____

_____

Significant Observations: _____

_____

Hike Rating: ☆☆☆☆☆

Gear Thoughts:

Food Thoughts:

Other Notes

Date:＿＿＿＿＿＿ Start Time:＿＿＿＿＿ End Time:＿＿＿＿＿

Weather: ☀ ☾ ☁ 🌧 ⚡ ❄ Temps:＿＿ Wind:＿＿

City/State/Country:＿＿＿＿＿＿＿＿＿＿＿＿＿＿＿

Trail(s)/Park:＿＿＿＿＿＿＿＿＿＿＿＿＿＿＿＿

Terrain:＿＿＿＿＿＿＿＿＿＿＿＿＿＿＿＿＿

Facilities:＿＿＿＿＿＿＿＿＿＿＿＿＿＿＿＿

Costs/Fees:＿＿＿＿＿＿＿＿＿＿＿＿＿＿＿

Cell Reception/Carrier:＿＿＿＿＿＿＿＿＿＿＿

Trail Type:　　　out/back　　　loop　　　one way/shuttle

Start Latitude/Longitude:＿＿＿＿＿＿＿＿＿

End Longitude/Latitude:＿＿＿＿＿＿＿＿＿

Elevation Gain/Loss:＿＿＿＿＿＿＿＿＿＿

Total Time:＿＿＿＿＿＿ Total Distance:＿＿＿＿＿

Trail Conditions:＿＿＿＿＿＿＿＿＿＿＿＿＿

Hiking Party:＿＿＿＿＿＿＿＿＿＿＿＿＿＿
＿＿＿＿＿＿＿＿＿＿＿＿＿＿＿＿＿＿＿＿＿

Significant Observations:＿＿＿＿＿＿＿＿＿＿
＿＿＿＿＿＿＿＿＿＿＿＿＿＿＿＿＿＿＿＿＿

Hike Rating: ☆ ☆ ☆ ☆ ☆

Gear Thoughts:

Food Thoughts:

Other Notes

Date:_____ Start Time:_____ End Time:_____

Weather: ☀ 🌤 🌧 ⛈ 🌨 Temps: Wind:

City/State/Country:_____

Trail(s)/Park:_____

Terrain:_____

Facilities:_____

Costs/Fees:_____

Cell Reception/Carrier:_____

Trail Type: out/back loop one way/shuttle

Start Latitude/Longitude:_____

End Longitude/Latitude:_____

Elevation Gain/Loss:_____

Total Time:_____ Total Distance:_____

Trail Conditions:_____

Hiking Party:_____
_____

Significant Observations:_____
_____

Hike Rating: ☆☆☆☆☆

Gear Thoughts:

Food Thoughts:

Other Notes

⛰ _____

Date: _____ Start Time: _____ End Time: _____

Weather: ☀ 🌙 🌧 ⛈ 🌨 Temps: _____ Wind: _____

City/State/Country: _____

Trail(s)/Park: _____

Terrain: _____

Facilities: _____

Costs/Fees: _____

Cell Reception/Carrier: _____

Trail Type: out/back   loop   one way/shuttle

Start Latitude/Longitude: _____

End Longitude/Latitude: _____

Elevation Gain/Loss: _____

Total Time: _____   Total Distance: _____

Trail Conditions: _____

Hiking Party: _____

_____

Significant Observations: _____

_____

Hike Rating: ☆ ☆ ☆ ☆ ☆

Gear Thoughts:

Food Thoughts:

Other Notes

Date:_____ Start Time:_____ End Time:_____

Weather: ☀ 🌙 🌧 ⛈ 🌨 Temps: Wind:

City/State/Country:_____

Trail(s)/Park:_____

Terrain:_____

Facilities:_____

Costs/Fees:_____

Cell Reception/Carrier:_____

Trail Type: out/back loop one way/shuttle

Start Latitude/Longitude:_____

End Longitude/Latitude:_____

Elevation Gain/Loss:_____

Total Time:_____ Total Distance:_____

Trail Conditions:_____

Hiking Party:_____

Significant Observations:_____

Hike Rating: ☆☆☆☆☆

Gear Thoughts: _____
_____
_____

Food Thoughts: _____
_____

Other Notes

_____
_____
_____
_____
_____
_____
_____
_____
_____
_____
_____
_____
_____
_____

Date:_____ Start Time:_____ End Time:_____

Weather: ☀ 🌙 🌧 ⚡ ❄ Temps:_____ Wind:_____

City/State/Country:_____

Trail(s)/Park:_____

Terrain:_____

Facilities:_____

Costs/Fees:_____

Cell Reception/Carrier:_____

Trail Type: out/back   loop   one way/shuttle

Start Latitude/Longitude:_____

End Longitude/Latitude:_____

Elevation Gain/Loss:_____

Total Time:_____   Total Distance:_____

Trail Conditions:_____

Hiking Party:_____

_____

Significant Observations:_____

Hike Rating: ☆☆☆☆☆

Gear Thoughts:

Food Thoughts:

Other Notes

Date:_____ Start Time:_____ End Time:_____

Weather: ☀ ☾ 🌧 ⛈ 🌨 Temps:_____ Wind:_____

City/State/Country:_____

Trail(s)/Park:_____

Terrain:_____

Facilities:_____

Costs/Fees:_____

Cell Reception/Carrier:_____

Trail Type: out/back   loop   one way/shuttle

Start Latitude/Longitude:_____

End Longitude/Latitude:_____

Elevation Gain/Loss:_____

Total Time:_____ Total Distance:_____

Trail Conditions:_____

Hiking Party:_____
_____

Significant Observations:_____
_____

Hike Rating: ☆ ☆ ☆ ☆ ☆

Gear Thoughts:

Food Thoughts:

Other Notes

Date:_____ Start Time:_____ End Time:_____

Weather: ☀ 🌙 🌧 ⚡ ❄ Temps:_____ Wind:_____

City/State/Country:_____

Trail(s)/Park:_____

Terrain:_____

Facilities:_____

Costs/Fees:_____

Cell Reception/Carrier:_____

Trail Type: out/back   loop   one way/shuttle

Start Latitude/Longitude:_____

End Longitude/Latitude:_____

Elevation Gain/Loss:_____

Total Time:_____ Total Distance:_____

Trail Conditions:_____

Hiking Party:_____

_____

Significant Observations:_____

_____

Hike Rating: ☆ ☆ ☆ ☆ ☆

Gear Thoughts: _____

_____

_____

Food Thoughts: _____

_____

_____

Other Notes

_____

_____

_____

_____

_____

_____

_____

_____

_____

_____

_____

_____

_____

_____

_____

Date:_____ Start Time:_____ End Time:_____

Weather: ☀ ☾ ☁ ⛈ ❄ Temps: Wind:

City/State/Country:_____

Trail(s)/Park:_____

Terrain:_____

Facilities:_____

Costs/Fees:_____

Cell Reception/Carrier:_____

Trail Type: out/back   loop   one way/shuttle

Start Latitude/Longitude:_____

End Longitude/Latitude:_____

Elevation Gain/Loss:_____

Total Time:_____   Total Distance:_____

Trail Conditions:_____

Hiking Party:_____

Significant Observations:_____

Hike Rating: ☆☆☆☆☆

Gear Thoughts: _____

_____

_____

Food Thoughts: _____

_____

_____

Other Notes

_____

_____

_____

_____

_____

_____

_____

_____

_____

_____

_____

_____

_____

_____

Date:_____ Start Time:_____ End Time:_____

Weather: ☀ ☾ ☁ ☁ ☁ Temps:_____ Wind:_____

City/State/Country:_____

Trail(s)/Park:_____

Terrain:_____

Facilities:_____

Costs/Fees:_____

Cell Reception/Carrier:_____

Trail Type: out/back   loop   one way/shuttle

Start Latitude/Longitude:_____

End Longitude/Latitude:_____

Elevation Gain/Loss:_____

Total Time:_____   Total Distance:_____

Trail Conditions:_____

Hiking Party:_____

_____

Significant Observations:_____

_____

Hike Rating: ☆ ☆ ☆ ☆ ☆

Gear Thoughts:

Food Thoughts:

Other Notes

Date:_____ Start Time:_____ End Time:_____

Weather: ☀ ☾ ☁ ⚡ ❄   Temps: Wind:

City/State/Country:_____

Trail(s)/Park:_____

Terrain:_____

Facilities:_____

Costs/Fees:_____

Cell Reception/Carrier:_____

Trail Type: out/back   loop   one way/shuttle

Start Latitude/Longitude:_____

End Longitude/Latitude:_____

Elevation Gain/Loss:_____

Total Time:_____   Total Distance:_____

Trail Conditions:_____

Hiking Party:_____

_____

Significant Observations:_____

Hike Rating: ☆☆☆☆☆

Gear Thoughts: _____
_____
_____

Food Thoughts: _____
_____
_____

Other Notes

_____
_____
_____
_____
_____
_____
_____
_____
_____
_____
_____
_____
_____
_____
_____

Date:_____ Start Time:_____ End Time:_____

Weather: ☀ ☾ 🌧 ☁ 🌨 Temps:_____ Wind:_____

City/State/Country:_____

Trail(s)/Park:_____

Terrain:_____

Facilities:_____

Costs/Fees:_____

Cell Reception/Carrier:_____

Trail Type: out/back   loop   one way/shuttle

Start Latitude/Longitude:_____

End Longitude/Latitude:_____

Elevation Gain/Loss:_____

Total Time:_____ Total Distance:_____

Trail Conditions:_____

Hiking Party:_____
_____

Significant Observations:_____
_____

Hike Rating: ☆ ☆ ☆ ☆ ☆

Gear Thoughts: _____

_____

_____

Food Thoughts: _____

_____

_____

Other Notes

_____

_____

_____

_____

_____

_____

_____

_____

_____

_____

_____

_____

_____

_____

_____

_____

Date:_____ Start Time:_____ End Time:_____

Weather: ☀ 🌙 🌧 ⛈ 🌨 Temps:_____ Wind:_____

City/State/Country:_____

Trail(s)/Park:_____

Terrain:_____

Facilities:_____

Costs/Fees:_____

Cell Reception/Carrier:_____

Trail Type: out/back   loop   one way/shuttle

Start Latitude/Longitude:_____

End Longitude/Latitude:_____

Elevation Gain/Loss:_____

Total Time:_____ Total Distance:_____

Trail Conditions:_____

Hiking Party:_____
_____

Significant Observations:_____
_____

Hike Rating: ☆ ☆ ☆ ☆ ☆

Gear Thoughts: _____

_____

_____

Food Thoughts: _____

_____

_____

Other Notes

_____

_____

_____

_____

_____

_____

_____

_____

_____

_____

_____

_____

_____

_____

⛰ _____

Date: _____ **Start Time:** _____ **End Time:** _____

Weather: ☀ 🌙 🌧 ⛈ 🌨 **Temps:** _____ **Wind:** _____

City/State/Country: _____

Trail(s)/Park: _____

Terrain: _____

Facilities: _____

Costs/Fees: _____

Cell Reception/Carrier: _____

Trail Type: out/back   loop   one way/shuttle

Start Latitude/Longitude: _____

End Longitude/Latitude: _____

Elevation Gain/Loss: _____

Total Time: _____ **Total Distance:** _____

Trail Conditions: _____

Hiking Party: _____

_____

Significant Observations: _____

_____

Hike Rating: ☆ ☆ ☆ ☆ ☆

Gear Thoughts: _____
_____
_____
_____

Food Thoughts: _____
_____
_____

Other Notes

_____
_____
_____
_____
_____
_____
_____
_____
_____
_____
_____
_____
_____
_____
_____

⛰ _____

Date:_____ Start Time:_____ End Time:_____

Weather: ☀ 🌙 🌧 ⚡ ❄   Temps:_____ Wind:_____

City/State/Country:_____

Trail(s)/Park:_____

Terrain:_____

Facilities:_____

Costs/Fees:_____

Cell Reception/Carrier:_____

Trail Type: out/back   loop   one way/shuttle

Start Latitude/Longitude:_____

End Longitude/Latitude:_____

Elevation Gain/Loss:_____

Total Time:_____ Total Distance:_____

Trail Conditions:_____

Hiking Party:_____

_____

Significant Observations:_____

_____

Hike Rating: ☆☆☆☆☆

Gear Thoughts:

Food Thoughts:

Other Notes

Date:_____ Start Time:_____ End Time:_____

Weather: ☀ ☾ 🌧 ⛈ ❄ Temps:_____ Wind:_____

City/State/Country:_____

Trail(s)/Park:_____

Terrain:_____

Facilities:_____

Costs/Fees:_____

Cell Reception/Carrier:_____

Trail Type: out/back   loop   one way/shuttle

Start Latitude/Longitude:_____

End Longitude/Latitude:_____

Elevation Gain/Loss:_____

Total Time:_____ Total Distance:_____

Trail Conditions:_____

Hiking Party:_____

Significant Observations:_____

Hike Rating: ☆ ☆ ☆ ☆ ☆

Gear Thoughts:

Food Thoughts:

Other Notes

Date:_____ Start Time:_____ End Time:_____

Weather: ☀ 🌙 🌧 ☁ 🌨 Temps:_____ Wind:_____

City/State/Country:_____

Trail(s)/Park:_____

Terrain:_____

Facilities:_____

Costs/Fees:_____

Cell Reception/Carrier:_____

Trail Type: out/back   loop   one way/shuttle

Start Latitude/Longitude:_____

End Longitude/Latitude:_____

Elevation Gain/Loss:_____

Total Time:_____ Total Distance:_____

Trail Conditions:_____

Hiking Party:_____

_____

Significant Observations:_____

Hike Rating: ☆☆☆☆☆

Gear Thoughts: _____
_____
_____

Food Thoughts: _____
_____
_____

Other Notes

_____
_____
_____
_____
_____
_____
_____
_____
_____
_____
_____
_____
_____
_____
_____

Date:_____ Start Time:_____ End Time:_____

Weather: ☀ 🌙 🌧 ⚡ ❄ Temps: Wind:

City/State/Country:_____

Trail(s)/Park:_____

Terrain:_____

Facilities:_____

Costs/Fees:_____

Cell Reception/Carrier:_____

Trail Type: out/back   loop   one way/shuttle

Start Latitude/Longitude:_____

End Longitude/Latitude:_____

Elevation Gain/Loss:_____

Total Time:_____ Total Distance:_____

Trail Conditions:_____

Hiking Party:_____

_____

Significant Observations:_____

_____

Hike Rating: ☆☆☆☆☆

Gear Thoughts: _____

_____

Food Thoughts: _____

_____

Other Notes

Date:_____ Start Time:_____ End Time:_____

Weather: ☀ 🌙 🌧 ⚡ ❄ Temps:_____ Wind:_____

City/State/Country:_____

Trail(s)/Park:_____

Terrain:_____

Facilities:_____

Costs/Fees:_____

Cell Reception/Carrier:_____

Trail Type: out/back   loop   one way/shuttle

Start Latitude/Longitude:_____

End Longitude/Latitude:_____

Elevation Gain/Loss:_____

Total Time:_____ Total Distance:_____

Trail Conditions:_____

Hiking Party:_____
_____

Significant Observations:_____
_____

Hike Rating: ☆☆☆☆☆

Gear Thoughts:

Food Thoughts:

Other Notes

Date:_____ Start Time:_____ End Time:_____

Weather: ☀ ☾ ⛅ 🌧 ⛈ 🌨 Temps:_____ Wind:_____

City/State/Country:_____

Trail(s)/Park:_____

Terrain:_____

Facilities:_____

Costs/Fees:_____

Cell Reception/Carrier:_____

Trail Type: out/back   loop   one way/shuttle

Start Latitude/Longitude:_____

End Longitude/Latitude:_____

Elevation Gain/Loss:_____

Total Time:_____   Total Distance:_____

Trail Conditions:_____

Hiking Party:_____

_____

Significant Observations:_____

Hike Rating: ☆☆☆☆☆

Gear Thoughts:_____

_____

_____

Food Thoughts:_____

_____

Other Notes

_____

_____

_____

_____

_____

_____

_____

_____

_____

_____

_____

_____

_____

_____

_____

Date:_____ Start Time:_____ End Time:_____

Weather: ☀ 🌙 🌧 ⛈ 🌨 Temps: Wind:

City/State/Country:_____

Trail(s)/Park:_____

Terrain:_____

Facilities:_____

Costs/Fees:_____

Cell Reception/Carrier:_____

Trail Type: out/back loop one way/shuttle

Start Latitude/Longitude:_____

End Longitude/Latitude:_____

Elevation Gain/Loss:_____

Total Time:_____ Total Distance:_____

Trail Conditions:_____

Hiking Party:_____

Significant Observations:_____

Hike Rating: ☆☆☆☆☆

Gear Thoughts: _____

_____

_____

Food Thoughts: _____

_____

_____

Other Notes

_____

_____

_____

_____

_____

_____

_____

_____

_____

_____

_____

_____

_____

_____

Date:_____ Start Time:_____ End Time:_____

Weather: ☀ ☾ ☁ ⚡ ❄   Temps:_____   Wind:_____

City/State/Country:_____

Trail(s)/Park:_____

Terrain:_____

Facilities:_____

Costs/Fees:_____

Cell Reception/Carrier:_____

Trail Type: out/back   loop   one way/shuttle

Start Latitude/Longitude:_____

End Longitude/Latitude:_____

Elevation Gain/Loss:_____

Total Time:_____   Total Distance:_____

Trail Conditions:_____

Hiking Party:_____

Significant Observations:_____

Hike Rating: ☆☆☆☆☆

Gear Thoughts:

Food Thoughts:

Other Notes

Date:_____ Start Time:_____ End Time:_____

Weather: ☀ 🌙 🌧 ⚡ ❄ Temps:_____ Wind:_____

City/State/Country:_____

Trail(s)/Park:_____

Terrain:_____

Facilities:_____

Costs/Fees:_____

Cell Reception/Carrier:_____

Trail Type: out/back   loop   one way/shuttle

Start Latitude/Longitude:_____

End Longitude/Latitude:_____

Elevation Gain/Loss:_____

Total Time:_____   Total Distance:_____

Trail Conditions:_____

Hiking Party:_____

_____

Significant Observations:_____

_____

Hike Rating: ☆ ☆ ☆ ☆ ☆

Gear Thoughts:_____

_____

_____

Food Thoughts:_____

_____

_____

Other Notes

_____

_____

_____

_____

_____

_____

_____

_____

_____

_____

_____

_____

_____

_____

_____

Date:_____ Start Time:_____ End Time:_____

Weather: ☀ ☾ ☁ ⚡ ❄ Temps:_____ Wind:_____

City/State/Country:_____

Trail(s)/Park:_____

Terrain:_____

Facilities:_____

Costs/Fees:_____

Cell Reception/Carrier:_____

Trail Type: out/back   loop   one way/shuttle

Start Latitude/Longitude:_____

End Longitude/Latitude:_____

Elevation Gain/Loss:_____

Total Time:_____ Total Distance:_____

Trail Conditions:_____

Hiking Party:_____

_____

Significant Observations:_____

_____

Hike Rating: ☆ ☆ ☆ ☆ ☆

Gear Thoughts:

_____

_____

_____

Food Thoughts:

_____

_____

_____

Other Notes

_____

_____

_____

_____

_____

_____

_____

_____

_____

_____

_____

_____

_____

_____

_____

_____

Date: _____ Start Time: _____ End Time: _____

Weather: ☀ ☾ ☁ ⛈ ❄   Temps: Wind:

City/State/Country: _____

Trail(s)/Park: _____

Terrain: _____

Facilities: _____

Costs/Fees: _____

Cell Reception/Carrier: _____

Trail Type: out/back   loop   one way/shuttle

Start Latitude/Longitude: _____

End Longitude/Latitude: _____

Elevation Gain/Loss: _____

Total Time: _____ Total Distance: _____

Trail Conditions: _____

Hiking Party: _____

_____

Significant Observations: _____

Hike Rating: ☆ ☆ ☆ ☆ ☆

Gear Thoughts:

_____

Food Thoughts:

_____

Other Notes

_____

Date:_____ Start Time:_____ End Time:_____

Weather: ☀ ☾ 🌧 ⚡ ❄   Temps:_____ Wind:_____

City/State/Country:_____

Trail(s)/Park:_____

Terrain:_____

Facilities:_____

Costs/Fees:_____

Cell Reception/Carrier:_____

Trail Type: out/back   loop   one way/shuttle

Start Latitude/Longitude:_____

End Longitude/Latitude:_____

Elevation Gain/Loss:_____

Total Time:_____ Total Distance:_____

Trail Conditions:_____

Hiking Party:_____

_____

Significant Observations:_____

_____

Hike Rating: ☆☆☆☆☆

Gear Thoughts:

Food Thoughts:

Other Notes

Date: _____ Start Time: _____ End Time: _____

Weather: ☀ 🌙 🌧 ⛈ 🌨 Temps: Wind:

City/State/Country: _____

Trail(s)/Park: _____

Terrain: _____

Facilities: _____

Costs/Fees: _____

Cell Reception/Carrier: _____

Trail Type: out/back   loop   one way/shuttle

Start Latitude/Longitude: _____

End Longitude/Latitude: _____

Elevation Gain/Loss: _____

Total Time: _____ Total Distance: _____

Trail Conditions: _____

Hiking Party: _____

Significant Observations: _____

Hike Rating: ☆☆☆☆☆

Gear Thoughts: _____

_____

Food Thoughts: _____

_____

Other Notes

_____

_____

_____

_____

_____

_____

_____

_____

_____

_____

_____

_____

_____

_____

Hike Log

Date: _____ Start Time: _____ End Time: _____

Weather: ☀ ☾ ☁ ⛈ ☁ Temps: _____ Wind: _____

City/State/Country: _____

Trail(s)/Park: _____

Terrain: _____

Facilities: _____

Costs/Fees: _____

Cell Reception/Carrier: _____

Trail Type: out/back   loop   one way/shuttle

Start Latitude/Longitude: _____

End Longitude/Latitude: _____

Elevation Gain/Loss: _____

Total Time: _____   Total Distance: _____

Trail Conditions: _____

Hiking Party: _____

_____

Significant Observations: _____

_____

Hike Rating: ☆ ☆ ☆ ☆ ☆

Gear Thoughts: _____

_____

_____

Food Thoughts: _____

_____

_____

Other Notes

_____

_____

_____

_____

_____

_____

_____

_____

_____

_____

_____

_____

_____

_____

_____

Date:_____ Start Time:_____ End Time:_____

Weather: ☀ ☾ 🌧 ⛈ ❄ Temps:_____ Wind:_____

City/State/Country:_____

Trail(s)/Park:_____

Terrain:_____

Facilities:_____

Costs/Fees:_____

Cell Reception/Carrier:_____

Trail Type: out/back   loop   one way/shuttle

Start Latitude/Longitude:_____

End Longitude/Latitude:_____

Elevation Gain/Loss:_____

Total Time:_____ Total Distance:_____

Trail Conditions:_____

Hiking Party:_____

_____

Significant Observations:_____

_____

Hike Rating: ☆☆☆☆☆

Gear Thoughts:

Food Thoughts:

Other Notes

Date:_____ Start Time:_____ End Time:_____

Weather: ☀ 🌙 🌧 ⚡ ❄ Temps: Wind:

City/State/Country:_____

Trail(s)/Park:_____

Terrain:_____

Facilities:_____

Costs/Fees:_____

Cell Reception/Carrier:_____

Trail Type: out/back   loop   one way/shuttle

Start Latitude/Longitude:_____

End Longitude/Latitude:_____

Elevation Gain/Loss:_____

Total Time:_____ Total Distance:_____

Trail Conditions:_____

Hiking Party:_____

_____

Significant Observations:_____

Hike Rating: ☆☆☆☆☆

Gear Thoughts: _____

_____

_____

Food Thoughts: _____

_____

_____

Other Notes

_____

_____

_____

_____

_____

_____

_____

_____

_____

_____

_____

_____

_____

_____

_____

Date:_____ Start Time:_____ End Time:_____

Weather: ☀ 🌙 🌧 ⚡ 🌨   Temps:_____ Wind:_____

City/State/Country:_____

Trail(s)/Park:_____

Terrain:_____

Facilities:_____

Costs/Fees:_____

Cell Reception/Carrier:_____

Trail Type: out/back   loop   one way/shuttle

Start Latitude/Longitude:_____

End Longitude/Latitude:_____

Elevation Gain/Loss:_____

Total Time:_____ Total Distance:_____

Trail Conditions:_____

Hiking Party:_____

_____

Significant Observations:_____

_____

Hike Rating: ☆☆☆☆☆

Gear Thoughts: _____
_____
_____

Food Thoughts: _____
_____
_____

Other Notes

_____
_____
_____
_____
_____
_____
_____
_____
_____
_____
_____
_____
_____
_____

Date:_____ Start Time:_____ End Time:_____

Weather: ☀ ☾ ☁ ⚡ ❄   Temps:_____ Wind:_____

City/State/Country:_____

Trail(s)/Park:_____

Terrain:_____

Facilities:_____

Costs/Fees:_____

Cell Reception/Carrier:_____

Trail Type: out/back   loop   one way/shuttle

Start Latitude/Longitude:_____

End Longitude/Latitude:_____

Elevation Gain/Loss:_____

Total Time:_____ Total Distance:_____

Trail Conditions:_____

Hiking Party:_____

_____

Significant Observations:_____

_____

Hike Rating: ☆ ☆ ☆ ☆ ☆

Gear Thoughts:

Food Thoughts:

Other Notes

Date:_____ Start Time:_____ End Time:_____

Weather: ☀ ☾ ☁ 🌧 ⛈ 🌨   Temps:_____   Wind:_____

City/State/Country:_____

Trail(s)/Park:_____

Terrain:_____

Facilities:_____

Costs/Fees:_____

Cell Reception/Carrier:_____

Trail Type: out/back   loop   one way/shuttle

Start Latitude/Longitude:_____

End Longitude/Latitude:_____

Elevation Gain/Loss:_____

Total Time:_____ Total Distance:_____

Trail Conditions:_____

Hiking Party:_____

_____

Significant Observations:_____

_____

Hike Rating: ☆☆☆☆☆

Gear Thoughts:

Food Thoughts:

Other Notes

Date:_____ Start Time:_____ End Time:_____

Weather: ☀ ☾ ☁ ⚡ ❄   Temps:_____ Wind:_____

City/State/Country:_____

Trail(s)/Park:_____

Terrain:_____

Facilities:_____

Costs/Fees:_____

Cell Reception/Carrier:_____

Trail Type: out/back   loop   one way/shuttle

Start Latitude/Longitude:_____

End Longitude/Latitude:_____

Elevation Gain/Loss:_____

Total Time:_____ Total Distance:_____

Trail Conditions:_____

Hiking Party:_____

_____

Significant Observations:_____

Hike Rating: ☆☆☆☆☆

Gear Thoughts:

Food Thoughts:

Other Notes

Manufactured by Amazon.ca
Acheson, AB